Podcasting with Youth

Podcasting with Youth

A QUICK GUIDE FOR LIBRARIANS
AND EDUCATORS

Lucas Maxwell

LIBRARIES
UNLIMITED®
An Imprint of ABC-CLIO, LLC
Santa Barbara, California • Denver, Colorado

Library of Congress Cataloging-in-Publication Data

Names: Maxwell, Lucas, author.
Title: Podcasting with youth : a quick guide for librarians and educators / Lucas Maxwell.
Description: First Edition. | Santa Barbara : Libraries Unlimited, 2020. | Includes bibliographical references and index.
Identifiers: LCCN 2020003262 (print) | LCCN 2020003263 (ebook) | ISBN 9781440870354 (Paperback : acid-free paper) | ISBN 9781440870361 (eBook)
Subjects: LCSH: Podcasting—Library applications. | Children's libraries—Activity programs.
Classification: LCC Z674.75.S63 M39 2020 (print) | LCC Z674.75.S63 (ebook) | DDC 006.7/52—dc23
LC record available at https://lccn.loc.gov/2020003262
LC ebook record available at https://lccn.loc.gov/2020003263

ISBN: 978-1-4408-7035-4 (paperback)
      978-1-4408-7036-1 (ebook)

24 23 22 21 20   1 2 3 4 5

This book is also available as an eBook.

Libraries Unlimited
An Imprint of ABC-CLIO, LLC

ABC-CLIO, LLC
147 Castilian Drive
Santa Barbara, California 93117
www.abc-clio.com

This book is printed on acid-free paper ∞

Manufactured in the United States of America

For Justine, for everything.

Contents

Conclusion 67

Acknowledgments

I'd like to thank the Student Library and Book Club team at Glenthorne High School for inspiring me on a daily basis and making going to work so much fun. Without you, the podcast would not exist and nor would this guide. To Nathalie for being an amazing library colleague. To Steve Ward for being a mentor, guide, and friend throughout the majority of my career at Glenthorne High School. I'd also like to thank everyone at ABC-CLIO for their constant support, patience and guidance. To Heather Moorefield-Lang for including me in numerous writing projects and for giving me the idea for this guide. And last but certainly not least, my wife Justine, and Jack and Lily, thank you for all of your patience and love.

Introduction

I have been working as a high school librarian in South London since 2013. Previous to this, I worked in the public library system as a teen services librarian in Nova Scotia, Canada, where I'm originally from, for five years.

Our podcast, Booklings Chat, was born out of an emergency. Not a real life or death emergency but one of those emergencies that only feels like life or death when you are in the moment. I had invited an author to Skype and had approximately seventy students crammed into the relatively small area that served as our library before we moved to a much more accommodating space.

While we were waiting for the author to log into Skype, I received an email from her. Her Skype had crashed and she wasn't able to connect with us. I could tell she felt terrible about it, and all of our efforts to troubleshoot via Twitter and email failed to fix the problem. The students, sitting on the floor, were watching my interactions with her on the library's Twitter feed as I had it projected for them to show them that we were doing everything we could to solve the problem. I was about to give up. I could feel the flop sweat forming at the back of my neck as I hadn't planned anything else for that lesson. I was fairly new to the job and having technology die on me in such a way.

Then, one of our book club members, who earlier in the year had helped come up with the name "Booklings" for the book club group, put her hand up.

"Why don't we ask her questions over Twitter?" Boom! Booklings Chat was born. We spent the next 30 minutes taking questions from the students, letting them come up to the laptop and write their questions down through the library's Twitter account.

It was a lot of fun, the students felt a real engagement with the author, and despite the fact that we weren't able to see her face to face, it turned into a great moment. From there, I decided to reach out to more and more authors, asking if they'd like to talk to our students over our lunch period for a 30-minute session. All I asked was that the authors use the hashtag #BooklingsChat when they responded so I could keep track of the conversation and archive it on a program like Wakelet. I will discuss how to archive these kinds of interactions later in this guide.

Our Twitter chats turned into an amazing way to reach out to authors that I knew would be difficult to bring into a school in London in person. These were typically American authors at first, but later I branched out to any author who was interested and this paid off. It introduced the authors to our students in a fun, easy way. The authors could engage in an informal way that didn't require too much of a time commitment. I would ask for 30 minutes, but if they had to cut it off at 20 it wasn't a problem. We would run these once a month in the library, and often they'd coincide with different events. These included days in which the school was focusing on well-being or mental health issues, upcoming holidays, or cultural events. We even had four authors talking to our students at once through Twitter to celebrate them being chosen for the BookTrust's (the United Kingdom's largest book charity) annual school library pack.

It was a huge hit with the students; they loved coming up to the computer to ask their questions. I'd have the lead student library assistants overseeing everything, taking questions in advance, and writing them down. It also helped us when it came time to ask for in-person author visits. Many of these authors had already talked to our book club students through Booklings Chat and therefore already had a relationship.

Sometimes, when we had a Twitter chat coming up, I'd ask students to come up with questions in advance using educational technology tools like Padlet. Padlet is a really great way to have teens share their ideas in one place. It looks like a virtual wall that can be designed by you or the teens. You can give them a unique and private security code, which they use to log in. They do not need to create an account, just you as the administrator. Once they are in they can add questions, thoughts, images, and even videos to the wall that appears in front of your admin screen in real time. You have the ability to vet everything before it goes up if that is a concern. Once you have the ideas, you can invite others to share or add. The uses of Padlet are vast; however, for Booklings Chat, we use it as a way to generate ideas for questions, what we used to call in high school a spit-balling question where ideas were just thrown up there for others to provide feedback for.

The ways I got the authors to take part were simple: I simply asked them on Twitter or via their website and any other channels that seemed appropriate. Authors are typically more than willing to engage with students—it's their audience. They don't always have enough time, and I completely understand why they can't constantly go out there and do things for free because this is their livelihood we're talking about. However, the Booklings Chat Twitter conversations helped set the stage for the podcast and probably wouldn't have existed without it.

Whatever kind of podcast you decide, I hope this guide will help you discover a few ways to get started, promote it effectively, and most importantly create a space for teens where they can use their imagination to make something they are proud of and have fun doing it.

In the following chapters, readers will learn several new things about podcasting. These include the benefits of podcasting, how to get a podcast started in the classroom and library, and how to generate interest in the project. Readers will also learn which podcasting equipment works best, at a wide variety of budgets, and tips on how to help your teens become better interviewers and presenters. Uploading your podcasting, marketing it, finding ideas to podcast about, and making it a fun and engaging project for you and your teens will conclude this guide.

Podcasting with Youth

Chapter 1

The Benefits of Podcasting

There are many ways podcasting can benefit not only teens but also the adults taking part in the program. If you're interested in starting a podcast, you might be in a position where you need to convince the powers that be to get one started, especially if you require some funding. I will discuss equipment and pricing in Chapter 3 of this guide, but money isn't the only topic to address when you approach your manager, principal, whomever, when you say you want to start a podcast with teens in the library or classroom.

It's important to highlight the benefits of this medium so you can get as many people on board as possible. The more people who are invested in your program, the more your teens will get out of it. I was fortunate that our teens won a grant to start their podcast. This gave us a lot of freedom when it came to purchasing equipment and getting started. As I'll discuss in Chapter 2, you do not need a huge budget to get your podcast off the ground. All you will need is some time and some dedicated teens. If you keep at it and try your best, you will then see your audience grow.

Below are just some of the benefits of podcasting that I've identified. These would be handy to keep note of if you are creating a plan to start a podcast and want to highlight its benefits to your manager.

Student-Created Content

No matter what kind of content you include in your podcast, it's important that the teens you work with are creating the content. We have a great team of podcasters, and I think of myself as their manager, someone who guides them along as they go, helps to edit when needed, and looks for new and exciting opportunities as they arise. Other than that, our students are generating the content on their own. For our podcast, students create interview questions before authors visit the school so they can be ready to interview them. They also are required to conduct some research on the author and look beyond the books that they write—for example, are there any political or social issues that the book covers? The teens can research this and develop well-informed questions far in advance.

There are, however, dozens of different ways to use podcasts in the library or classroom. When students are in control of the podcast, you are telling them that you value their input and that they have ownership over a specific aspect of the library, classroom, or wherever you decide to record.

Reach New Audiences

Creating a school-based or public library podcast is an amazing way to put your school or library on the map in a positive, engaging way. If you decide to use it in the classroom as a way to reflect on learning, parents can easily access it and learn more about their teens' education journey. If you endeavor to highlight school achievements, there's no better way than to broadcast it out in a podcast. If your goal is to bring new faces to the library, a podcast is a way to attract teens who may have a stereotypical view of what libraries can offer. You'll also be able to draw in new teachers if you work in a school library and new staff and members of the public if you are in the public library sector. In addition, you can connect with a worldwide audience, introducing the teens to other like-minded students.

I will discuss specific ways to use podcasts in your library or classroom later in this chapter, but for reaching a new audience and introducing your school or library to the world, podcasting is one of the most effective methods there is.

Podcasts Are Flexible

The great thing about podcasts is that they can be listened to at any juncture; there's no time requirement, you don't need to travel anywhere, and content is easily consumed. Our podcast is hosted on SoundCloud, which can be easily accessed on an app or through the library's website. Your teens simply need to worry about creating a great, listenable podcast that will engage their audience, and it will grow from there. I will discuss different podcasting platforms and step-by-step instructions on how to upload, access, and make the most out of them in a later chapter. What's important to remember is that a podcast offers you and the teens you are working with a lot of flexibility. Your listeners can access it at their leisure, and once you've created a publishing schedule, you will be able to follow along at a pace that they choose.

Editing Is Easy

Editing audio is so much simpler than editing video. I will discuss equipment in Chapter 3, but it's crucial that you have the appropriate equipment and programs to create a high-quality-sounding podcast. Doing this will not break the bank and will help spread your teens' work around the world. Editing doesn't have to be as tedious as it sounds; in fact, there is such a thing as too much editing. You don't have to worry about creating "the best" podcast ever made. What's crucial is that you give teens the tools they need to edit themselves and let them work on it until they are happy. Remember, with all of the programs I will discuss, there is always an "undo" button ready and waiting to be clicked. Nothing has to be permanent—it's not the end of the world if it doesn't sound like the most downloaded podcast on iTunes. Let the teens make something they are proud of, let them have fun, let them learn and create, and a great product will follow.

Connects the Students

Our podcasting team has interviewed over twenty authors since we've started, and the teens have made several connections, friends, and confidants. One of our podcast team members has written her own young adult novel, and many of the authors we've spoken to have offered to read it and provide feedback.

Interviewing these authors has also resulted in some very exciting and unique opportunities. In June 2019, our podcast caught the attention of Penguin Publishing here in the United Kingdom, and one of our teens was asked to interview author Malorie Blackman at the London Palladium in front of close to 3,000 people. This was an experience that she'll never forget. It wouldn't have happened if we hadn't decided to start the podcast with little to no equipment, experience, or any idea what we were doing. We took a chance, we learned together, and it paid off in ways that can't really be measured. My advice to anyone hesitant to start something like a podcast is to just dive in and try it because you never know where it's going to lead you.

Screen-Time Reduction

Too much screen time is a big concern for both parents and educators. Podcasting is a great alternative to screens because not only are teens engaging their minds in ways that video games and social media can't offer, but they are also thinking critically, resting their eyes, and creating content that is uniquely their own. It's a high-tech program without a screen, something that is rare in today's society. Podcasting harkens back to the "olden" days of radio; depending on what kind of show they produce, podcasting can take teens into a new world where exciting new opportunities are available.

Teaching New Skills

I have witnessed my students learn several new skills when it comes to their podcasting experience. First, they've learned teamwork skills by working together to create a schedule as to who interviews who when, who operates the equipment, and who creates the interview questions. They've also learned to be diplomatic when it comes to interviewing guests who are popular, which could potentially create tension when more than one student is interested in sitting in on the interview. Luckily, we have a very mature group of students, and this hasn't been an issue, and it's something I'm very proud of as I've watched them grow as a team.

The speaking skills on the part of the teens have greatly increased. By listening back to their recordings, they are able to reflect on their tone and clarity. They can then go back and try to improve on this the next time they record. I will discuss interviewing and podcasting skills in Chapter 4, but by learning through trial and error, students have been able to correct any repetitive mistakes they may have made and in turn become more confident and clearer speakers. I would describe more than one member of our podcast team as an introvert, teens who may not necessarily enjoy being in the spotlight or standing up in front of a group of people and speaking about a certain topic. Podcasting allows teens to express themselves, talk openly about issues that are important to them and ask serious, engaging questions without the pressure of being in front of an audience. It is an amazing transitional tool that builds their confidence in public speaking incrementally.

The teens' confidence has grown tremendously over the past year. I've seen them go from shy, introverted (at least some of them) to outgoing and expressive teens. Being put on the spot with an author or guest and asking them questions can be intimidating for a teen, but over time I've noticed that their nerves have gradually melted away. This kind of confidence will not be restricted to podcasting but will carry over into their school and social lives. It may also pique their interest in media, interviewing, or broadcasting and send them down a path to a future career. I see my job as providing these opportunities, and podcasting delivers on several fronts.

In addition to all of this, podcasting has helped the teens and myself become better listeners. We try hard to create a show that is conversational in tone, and to do this, our team needs to ask questions and listen to the author's response before jumping in with the next question. This may seem obvious, but when the red "record" button is on and you've got an author sitting in front of you and your headphones are on, it's another story. Good listening skills don't often come naturally, and I'm very happy to see how my team and I have both progressed in this department.

The teens have also learned several technical skills. Learning to operate the equipment carries with it a sharp learning curve for many, especially if you haven't encountered the programs before. I have learned several new skills as well that I wouldn't have even considered engaging with before. The students learn to edit, record, broadcast, and publish their podcast. They also learn about the importance of marketing their podcast and creating content that is attractive and listenable. They use their artistic skills and graphic design programs to create a professional-looking podcast through logos, posters with quotes from the authors, and bookmarks. They use their musical skills to come up with songs that will be used in the opening and closing credits of each podcast.

Creates a Safe Environment

When I was a student in high school, and I know this isn't everyone's experience, you could become a target if you showed too much enthusiasm for anything labeled "geeky" or "uncool." Having a safe place like a library or a classroom with a teacher who is invested in the program can create more than just a place to record voices. It can become a refuge for many students. A place where they can dive into their interests with like-minded people without fear of judgment or mockery can make a huge difference in a teen's life. This brings me to my next point.

It's a Place Where Mistakes Are Okay

It's not the end of the world if the podcast doesn't sound professional on the first take. That's what editing is for. It doesn't matter if it takes them thirty attempts to get the intro to the podcast right. Let them have fun, let them make mistakes, let them learn together. They will have been in school all day long, many of them worrying about making mistakes, ticking the wrong box, saying the wrong thing, wearing the wrong clothes, giving the wrong answer. The podcast environment should be a place where none of this matters, where all are welcome and mistakes are laughed at, and you move on. Failing is such an important part of life, especially the teenage life. It teaches them responsibility, coping skills, and how to adapt. Perhaps most importantly, it teaches them not to be afraid of failure. Chris Hudson (2012) states that:

> In a world that is obsessed with teaching young people the *correct* way to do things, we risk creating a generation who are focused on not getting things wrong rather than on really understanding or exploring ideas. Letting young people have the freedom to fail and to make mistakes empowers them to explore their creativity, to learn real lessons, and develop a deeper understanding of the world and who they are. If we teach our young people the only thing that matters is not making mistakes we channel and restrict their thinking. They spend so much of their energy pleasing others and trying to conform that they lose their desire to create, dream, and discover new ways of seeing the world and themselves.

Inspires Students to Look Further

Creating a podcast, or creating anything in a fun, safe environment where failure is taught to be accepted instead of a disaster, can help improve student curiosity and well-being.

Questions that students might have in the classroom or other areas of their lives but are too shy or hesitant to ask can now be explored with their friends in a nonjudgmental atmosphere. There is a great deal of exploration when it comes to creating a podcast, generating ideas, creating the "brand," and much more. Yes, there are "black and white" aspects to the technical side of podcasting, but once you've got these nailed down, the teens can then move on to investigation, finding solutions and a system that works for their podcast. It can be a truly rewarding program if you give them the right tools to get started.

Helps Teens Think Differently

There are so many things going on in creating a podcast—technical needs, questions, atmosphere, teamwork, broadcasting skills, and more. Having teens run a podcast in your school or library will help them think differently when it comes to problem solving. This is a valuable tool to have and one that might not come across in the classroom. I'm not disparaging the school system in any way, but rather I'm highlighting the fact that creating a podcast can provide unexpected benefits that will carry over into the teens' school and personal lives.

Enriches Conversation and Presentation Skills

The goal of most podcasts is to create an environment where the interview or discussion comes across as a relaxed, informal conversation. This takes time, but with practice I've noticed the teens I work with developing these skills. There is no doubt in my mind that this will translate to future presentations and conversations they will have with their peers, teachers, parents, and future employers.

Creates a Real-World Connection

Something we hear all the time is: "I'll never use what I did in school in the 'real world.'" Podcasting is something that again, will carry over into whatever becomes the real world for these teens when they finish school. Seeing how their hard work and determination, practice, and resilience can create something real and tangible that can potentially last forever is a testament to this. These teens may do the podcast for a while and decide it's not for them, but for some, it might hit the right note and become their world. It might open a door for them that they weren't aware even existed.

We also often hear people say that they forget what they learned in school the moment they're finished with the assignment. This isn't the case with a podcast because it requires teens to use hands-on skills that they can apply, use, and create a tangible result. They are not relying on rote memory; they are creating something with their peers, using new skills and developing their own voice, something that they will use for the rest of their lives.

There are several benefits to podcasting; in my experience the students involved in this project learn continuously, as do I. The important thing to remember is to keep trying and not to feel overwhelmed by the idea of getting started. Take small steps, learn as you go, and have fun!

Key Takeaways

- Podcasting teaches students several new skills including interviewing, public speaking, teamwork, and technical skills. It also teaches students to be better listeners, something that is crucial when it comes to being a good interviewer.
- Students learn that making mistakes is acceptable and part of the learning process.
- Podcasting in the library or classroom creates a fun, safe environment where it's okay to "geek out."
- Podcasting creates opportunities and skills that can be applied to future career goals and interests of the students.

Chapter 2

Getting Started

Getting started with a podcast may seem overwhelming. I know I felt slightly overwhelmed even after our teens won a grant to start their own. I didn't know what to do, what equipment to buy, or even if I'd be able to recruit enough teens to keep it going on a regular basis. After a lot of trial and error, I'm happy to say that we now have a team that keeps things running superbly. This chapter will go over some strategies on how to start a podcast, develop interest on the part of teens and staff members, and create something memorable.

As with any library program, ensure you have full permission from your manager, principal, head teacher, or whoever oversees your performance in the setting that you work in to start a podcast. We'll talk about budgeting for equipment in the next chapter, but it's important that those in your Finance Department and your manager are aware of the cost of the podcast and the amount of time it will consume on your part and on the part of the students.

Before you can think about any of this, though, you have to know if your students or teens are interested in the project at all. It's crucial that you put some feelers out there and advertise. Set up a meeting. Does your public library have a Teen Advisory Board? Do you have student library assistants in your school? If so, make heavy use of them. They may be interested in starting a podcast themselves or can put you in touch with students who will be interested.

If you're thinking of starting one in your classroom, here are a few things to consider: Ask the students what kinds of things they are interested in outside of school. As a librarian, I'm constantly asking teens who claim they hate reading what kinds of video games, TV shows, sports, or YouTube channels they follow. This is often a great way to recommend a book that might hook them. The same goes for podcasting. Find a hook—find something that will keep them interested and coming back for more.

My students enjoy interviewing people, specifically authors when they visit the library or via the phone if they are too far away to visit. Whatever it is, the students must really enjoy the topic. If the subject is something they don't care about, this will shine through in the recording. The thing to remember is that at the beginning, you'll likely have no one listening, so you better be passionate about whatever it is you're talking about when those first listeners do strap in and start checking out your material.

You'll also want to think about what kind of format to create. Will the students interview each other or guests to the school or library? Will it simply be a discussion among each other? If so, ensure there is a common theme or thread running through each one. Will the students want to create their own stories like radio shows from the past? Will they want to do nonfiction stories (think serial, true crime, investigations, etc.), or you may find it's simply one student riffing on a specific topic or area of interest.

It's known that interview podcasts are the most popular, followed by looser, conversational-type podcasts, and then followed by educational shows (Prangley, 2017).

Another thing to consider is what you want the students to get out of it. When we started the podcast, my goal was to get students interviewing authors when they visited the school solely because I thought it was a unique and interesting thing to do, and the students were really excited about doing it. Over time, my goal went a little deeper. I wanted their confidence to rise, I wanted to teach them technical skills. I wanted them to become great broadcasters, writers, and interviewers. I wanted them to learn skills that they could take with them for the rest of their lives. Our podcast has been running for a year now, and I hope we've achieved at least some of those goals.

If you're in the classroom, you'll want to ensure the podcast is relevant to the students' learning. If your podcast doesn't have a focus, the students may not be as on board as they should be, which could result in the entire program going off the rails.

Getting Started in the Classroom

There are many ways to get started using podcasting in the classroom. Here are a few ways you, as a teacher, could get the most out of podcasting. Murray (2019) provides several effective methods, including:

1. Having students record a tour of the school. This can then be played to new students as they walk around and get to know their new setting. This can be done throughout the school or in smaller settings like the library. There are many aspects to a busy library that many students may find intimidating or overwhelming. Having a library intro podcast would be a huge benefit to new students. This could include how the library is laid out, how long they can borrow books, the library's hours, how to go about creating a reservation list, who the student library assistants are, and more. This might work even better as a vlog or straight-up video; however, a podcast would be a great place to start.
2. When important cultural events are on the horizon, students can podcast what it means to them and share this with parents and the entire school. This approach does not have to be long; it could be played in classrooms given the correct

technology or over a PA system. It's just one way that podcasting can give students their own voice on the issues that
are important to them.

3.   Students can deliver weekly podcasts on current events and
      news stories that they are interested in. Teens are more tuned
      in to the news than we give them credit for. With today's frag-
      mented media landscape and misleading news headlines
      making their way into social media and other outlets, having
      students report on authentic, responsibly researched news sto-
      ries as a podcast would be an amazing project to get off the
      ground.

4.   Students can podcast debates. At Glenthorne High School, we
      have debates in the library occasionally, and they are a lot of
      fun. It hadn't occurred to me that I could use the podcast to
      share the debate. Our last debate focused on young adult lit-
      erature, whether or not teens felt accurately represented in the
      literature that they read. If we had been operating the pod-
      cast at this point, it would have been a great way to bring our
      podcast into the world. I highly recommend getting into
      debating even if you decide podcasting isn't for you. Record-
      ing a debate as a podcast is also an amazing way for the debat-
      ers to listen and reflect on what went well and what they
      could improve on.

5.   Bringing in guest speakers (this is the current format for our
      podcast, Booklings Chat). These can be hosted and stored
      online (which I'll explain in later chapters) for students who
      are absent or classes in the future.

6.   Have students interview each other and other teachers. This
      is not something I've done to a huge extent, but I think it would
      really break down potential barriers that might exist between
      students and teachers and clear up confusion. An idea I have
      for the end of the year is to interview Year 7 (age 11) students
      in July when they are about to go into Year 8. We will ask them
      what they wish they had known when they first started at our
      school. This can help us as librarians and other teachers to
      guide and assist new students as they come to the school,
      often from a small primary school into what is a very large
      and busy high school.

7.   Have students interested in music create a podcast focused on
      a specific instrument or song.

8.   Alternative to book reports: Have students record their book
      talks or reports within the podcast. This could be done easily
      as a weekly podcast, having a certain number of students
      recording a five-minute-each podcast on a specific book. It
      doesn't have to be only book reports; it can be for any

presentation and has the potential to connect you to other departments in the school.

9. Students can use the podcast like roving reporters or interviewers, getting details about important sporting, musical, or dramatic events and putting them down as a podcast. The goal would be to do these fairly often as they would date quickly.

GradeSlam (2015) has a very interesting way to use podcasting in the classroom: Have students use a podcast to document their research assignment. At Glenthorne, several of our Year 8 (age 12) students undergo a research project on a topic of their choice. The idea behind it is to teach them how to recognize and avoid plagiarism, research responsibly, create a bibliography, and understand the importance of leaving a positive digital footprint. We had them use a program called Flipgrid to reflect on their research. They recorded a video discussing what their topic was and what they hoped to learn. As they progressed through the project, they discussed what sources they were using and why, any challenges they were experiencing, and how they felt the project was going. I would love to try this as a podcast in the future; students can record a podcast every two weeks and update their teachers, parents, and classmates on their progress.

The research podcasts wouldn't have to be long, 5 minutes each, having students thinking critically on their topics. Students could also discuss and provide feedback on other students' research. This would be an amazing way for students to learn and build on ideas that their peers provide.

You'll also want to think about what you'll expect of your students. It depends on the age range, but it's important to know that even with an unlimited budget, your podcast probably isn't going to sound like a truly professional one. There's nothing wrong with that. It's crucial not to lay too heavy an expectation on the students before you start. Let them listen to a wide variety of podcasts. I told my students that we'd simply do our best, edit what we could, and not worry about little hiccups. We learned along the way, and the students' editing skills have improved as well as their interview skills.

In my experience, the best way to get youth involved in any kind of library program is to promote it as much as humanly possible. The same goes for podcasting—promotion is the key to getting students involved. That, and food.

First, decide on what age students you'd like to get involved with the podcast. Do you want to target a specific grade, or do you want a mixture of ages? For our podcast, we have Year 10 students (Grade 9 equivalent), and they are primarily girls. This isn't something I aimed for—it's just who ended up being the most interested and involved in the program. As the team gets older, and school exams become more pressing, challenging, and stressful, I know that I will have to recruit new students to the podcast in the coming years.

My advice is to ensure you have a core group of older students who possess some technical knowledge that they can pass down to the younger less experienced students. It's also a built-in mentoring system—the older students can train the younger ones. The younger students can observe the older students interviewing people who visit the school or even each other and learn valuable skills in the process. In turn, the older students are learning new skills and developing their leadership, teamwork, technical, and organization skills. This will also assist with retaining students and recruiting them for future podcasts. You might want to bring in "special guests": students who come in as one-off to promote a specific topic or idea. Your podcast should be about what the students want it to be about. The podcast we run is mainly about books because that's what the students who run it are interested in. This doesn't mean your podcast has to be about the novels they are reading; it can be about their favorite movies, news, and politics or simply ideas they'd like to see get off the ground.

As the official administrator, your role is to provide them with the equipment and the initial know-how. However, if you have a core group of mature teens at the helm, you won't have to stress about content. Teens have a lot to say, they are much more empathetic and tuned in than many outside of the teaching or library profession give them credit for. The podcast can be a way to give them a voice that may be eluding them.

In a school setting, promoting the podcast involves visiting homerooms, assemblies, and classes to get the word out to the students. I used a few simple slides, almost no text, just a few photos with the times and dates that they could meet in the library to discuss an exciting new program that involved podcasting.

Speak to them when they come into the library, or go and visit them in smaller groups in the classroom. Have a flyer at your desk that you can hand out. I don't know how I'd live without a program like Canva to create cool-looking flyers, posters, and bookmarks. It's a free program with really amazing features. I don't work for them or get paid to say that—I really do rely on it on a daily basis. I should mention that once you have a group of students interested in the program, it's a good idea to let them come up with the name, logo, and all advertising for your podcast. Other alternatives to Canva are Lucidpress, Snappa, Stencil, and Tailor Brands.

To promote it even more, have students place posters in the cafeterias, in bathrooms, and wherever they are allowed. If your school has video or audio announcements or screens throughout the school, you can also make use of those.

Make use of your student library assistants if you have them. I am very fortunate in that I have ten dedicated students who are more than happy to visit lunch lines, basketball courts, playgrounds, and courtyards to spread the word. When student library assistants are checking books out to students, have them place a premade bookmark with the podcast program in their book.

The idea is to get a lot of students involved at the beginning because without fail some students will lose interest and drop away from the program. It's nothing to be offended by; in my ten years of teen library programming, I've gotten more than used to seeing teens come and go. Their interests can vary widely, their schedules may be already overwhelming, or they just may feel that podcasting isn't for them.

Book displays also work. Create a display using books that feature podcasts and music in them like *Radio Silence* by

Alice Oseman or *Nick & Norah's Infinite Playlist* by David Levithan and Rachel Cohn to attract attention to the program.

If you have a whiteboard, ask students what their favorite podcasts are. I tried this and was pleased to discover that a small handful of students were mildly obsessed with *Welcome to Nightvale*. They really wanted the podcast to take a similar direction: providing updates for a fictional school, wherein the updates get more and more surreal and strange. I loved the idea; however, it didn't end up working out in the end.

Alternatively, ask students if they'd be interested in a podcast program. I tried this before I started our Dungeons & Dragons program with the message: Should we start a Dungeons & Dragons program? I had three columns: Yes, No, and What's Dungeons & Dragons. There was an overwhelming number of check marks in the "Yes" column, so we started it up once a week, and now it runs twice a week with two separate dungeon masters. The "What's Dungeons & Dragons" column also had a few ticks until one student wrote over it "It's that game from Stranger Things!" which, in hindsight, probably would have saved me a lot of time in gauging how well the students knew about the program.

If you're lucky enough that teachers bring in students for library lessons or research-based classes, use this time to promote the podcast and to gauge interest. Reaching out to parents is also a good idea. I try to sit on a few parent council meetings every year to promote big-ticket events, and it usually pays off. If you have a social media presence, create a hashtag around your podcast or let the students create one once they've chosen a name.

Creating a Name for the Podcast

Our podcast was created by members of our book club, who meet once a week at lunch and call themselves the Booklings. They came up with Booklings Chat for the name of the podcast; therefore, the hashtag #BooklingsChat is what we use to promote it on social media and all of our bookmarks, flyers, and posters.

Coming up with a name can be one of the hardest things to do when creating a podcast. Podcasts like *Rationally Speaking, You Are Not So Smart,* and *The Memory Palace* are all great names. They are attention grabbing and expand on historical topics, psychological issues, and rational thinking. It's important that the name reflect the style and substance of the show in some respect. Booklings Chat works for us because it has the word "Book" in the title, is the name of our book club, and is unique. You'll want to search in iTunes and Google to ensure that your podcast name hasn't already been taken.

Making Space Online

If you have a blog, create a separate page to promote and highlight the podcast. Blog about your experience setting it up; have students blog and reflect on it once they've been doing it a little while. Ask if you can send the blog out to parents or if you have a group email or SMS system at your school; ask if you can use this to send a message out to grades that you think would be the most interested. Go as wide as you can, see who sticks it out, and then you can work on a schedule.

Seek Partnership

If you have a dedicated Media Department, visit them and see which students might be interested in starting a podcast. They might already have one set up or are also interested in starting one. Our podcast was the start of a beautiful friendship with our Media Department; they have been extremely helpful with advice on setting up the podcast. They alone may have the expertise on how to start one.

It's also useful to visit your Music and IT Departments to discuss equipment. I had our music technician provide advice on the sort of microphones, recorders, and software to use (see Chapter 3 for this information), and it saved me a huge amount of time in getting set up. I was fortunate in that I already had a great relationship with the Music Department because when I started at Glenthorne High School in 2013, one of the first programs that I started on a monthly basis was an Open Mic for the students. This required asking someone from that department to teach me how to set up the equipment and which equipment was required. Eventually, I was able to book it out and set it up myself. With the help of the Open Mic students, we'd travel to the Music Department, collect it, and set it up. This meant I was no longer requiring as much assistance from the department, although I still relied on them for tech issues.

Speaking in staff meetings and briefings will not only get staff who might be interested in helping out involved, but it will also prompt them to tell students who they think would benefit from the opportunity.

If you're in a public library, set up a visit with your local middle or high school. Schedule a meeting with their librarian (if they have one), media technician or teacher, or Music Department to tell them about your idea. They will be able to put you in touch with students who are keen to take part. Bring a flyer or other promotional items to hand out, and put them on their bulletin boards and in their library.

Use existing programs that already bring in teens, such as the aforementioned Teen Advisory Board, craft programs, anything where you're working with teens on a regular basis. Ensure the program is advertised heavily in your Teen Section if you're fortunate enough to have one. As I've already mentioned, our podcast was born out of an idea from a mixture of our book club and student library assistants. Without these programs existing I wouldn't' have known a podcast was something that they wanted to take part in.

Creating Shared Expectations

With a podcast, it's a good idea to have a few meetings before you get started. This is a good way to ensure everyone is on the same page. Bring food. I might be preaching to the choir with this statement, but food is without doubt the best way to attract teens to a specific program. Pizza is the best in my opinion. Krispy Kreme Doughnuts comes in second, followed by any kind of chocolate. They will come, they will sit, and they will listen—it has never failed me.

From these meetings you can determine what the podcast's primary aim will be. What will the podcast focus on? The podcast I run in the library focuses on young adult novels. The students interview authors when they visit the school. The students also podcast as a group together, discussing their favorite books and which books they hope to read in the future.

Although students can run a podcast on any topic, it's up to you to help guide them to something that will keep them motivated and coming back to the library to take part.

If you have students who are interested in a specific genre, it might be a good idea to invite them to take part in the podcast. I have a large group of students, mainly 12–13-year-olds who share an obsession with Manga, Anime, and other aspects of Japanese culture, and I am in the process of getting them to record an episode on what they are reading. Any librarian who stocks Manga knows that students can fly through a volume a day at least. I know that my library could be stocked entirely with Manga, and it still wouldn't be enough to hold down the voracious appetite these students have. I could write an entire chapter on how I started our Manga Club and how popular it has become. With the podcast and with any library program, it's vital that you get to know your students' interests; that way you will make it something they will want to invest in, rather than something you spend time trying to get them interested in.

For our podcast, we have close to ten students who are part of the podcast team. They work on a rotation system. Two students get to interview an author or a special guest when they visit the school. A third student keeps an eye on the recorder, mixer levels, microphones, and microphone stands (more on equipment in Chapter 3). I can't tell you the number of times we've relied on this third student to catch a microphone stand that wasn't tightened properly or to turn down a dial on the recorder so that the volume levels weren't skewed. That said, it's a learning process for everyone, it's not going to be perfect, and that's okay. It is, however, going to be (hopefully) a lot of fun and something that students can take ownership over.

The next time an author or special guest visits, another two students do the interview, and so on. Of course, authors and special guests aren't coming to the school or library every week, so it's important that the students record an episode on a weekly basis if they can. We'll have three or four students set it up and discuss what they're reading and what books or movies they're looking forward to. The next week, another three or four will come in and do the same. This way, you get three weeks of podcasts ready to go before the next group comes in. As previously mentioned, the podcast team I work with are members of our book club and are very avid readers. After three weeks, they will have more books to discuss.

Creating a Schedule

Whatever theme you decide on, it's important that you create a schedule and stick to it as best as you can. Consistency is key, once you know how often you will record, sit down and decide how often you will post your recording (more on how to actually post a recording in Chapter 3).

If you want to try for weekly, ensure you have a bank of podcasts already recorded before you do so in case life gets in the way and you can't get everyone together to record. Post your schedule somewhere visible; these teens will most likely be regulars to your library, and it will be a good reminder for them.

If you work in a school, set up an email group for the students, and remind them on a weekly basis whose turn it is to come in. You may need to schedule this during their breaks or lunches or before and after school. Doing this will ensure you get the most committed students. Pulling them out of classes will be popular, but you run the risk of attracting students who are just there to get out of class. This is something that you'll be able to gauge pretty quickly.

When I worked in a public library, I had a dedicated group of teens who worked with younger students for a literacy-based program once a week. I set up an email system with their homeroom teacher and librarian to help remind them. It took some time developing the relationship, visiting the school, assisting with their library programs, and meeting the students, but it paid off in the end.

Once you've got your core team, you're ready to roll with the podcast. You might decide to purchase the equipment before you even have your first meeting. This will work, but you may find yourself storing it away until you find your team. My approach was to create the team first, because, as you'll find out in the next chapter, recording your first podcast doesn't require a ton of fancy equipment. The important thing to focus on, in my opinion, is to get the students together discussing things that are important to them.

Getting started on your podcast can seem overwhelming at first, but it doesn't have to feel this way. Reach out to other departments if you're in a school or other experts if you're in a public library. Ask your more able teen library users to help you create a name, navigate the tech, and create a space online. By creating an expectation among your podcast team, it will ensure they take the project seriously, which will result in a more polished product.

Key Takeaways

- Choose the right kind of podcast for your classroom or library. Interview podcasts are the most popular; however, you can use them to highlight school achievements, research projects, current events, debates, whatever you want.
- Having a core group of older students to assist younger ones will decrease workload for you as the administrator while teaching students valuable leadership and teamwork skills.
- Seek partnerships with other departments, the Media and Music Departments can typically assist with setting up the podcast and teaching the students the basics if needed.
- Have students create a schedule and ensure they stick to it. Creating expectations around who is in charge of what is key to a successful podcast.
- Have students create a name for the podcast and develop any of the artwork if possible; having this led by students makes it something they will own and be proud of.

Chapter 3

Podcasting Equipment

Starting a podcast and trying to understand what kind of equipment to use can be an intimidating process. However, recording a podcast doesn't have to be expensive. Library budgets are tight and in some cases nearly nonexistent. Luckily, you can have your students recording their thoughts, ideas, and interviews in a relatively short time for little money. In this chapter I'm going to discuss many different equipment types and their price ranges. I will also discuss different ways to record your podcast on multiple devices.

Essentially, all you need to record a podcast is a computer and a microphone. This could be a simple USB microphone that you hook up to your PC. You can purchase a CMTECK USB microphone on Amazon for $20. If you'd like to go even cheaper, Jounivo makes a USB microphone for $12.99. If you'd like to splurge a little more, Alvoxcon makes a wireless USB microphone for $37.99. One of the best USB microphones on the market is the Audio-Technica ATR2100. It will cost you around $70 on Amazon. It has a built-in audio jack, so you can hear yourself recording if that is something you'd like to experience. If you want to go even higher, the Samson Q2U USB and XLR microphone will be around $95 and is an amazing microphone.

No matter what microphone you choose, it's a good idea to purchase a set of headphones, so you can hear yourself and drown out any other noise in the room. There are so many different options out there and like anything, price ranges are varied. If you prefer earbuds over the large ones that are considered over-ear, you can purchase the Panasonic HJE120 Earbuds for approximately $20. There aren't many better ear-buds out there for that low of a price. You could have multiple pairs for the teens in your group. If you're still hooked on earbuds but are willing to spend some more money, the Sony XBA-C10IP Earbuds will run you around $53.

If you're still looking to save money but still have a decent set of over-ear headphones, the Behringer HPS3000 Studio Headphones will get the job done and cost you approximately $20 on Amazon. Next up you can purchase the Lyx-Pro Has-10 Over-Ear headphones for $40. They aren't too fancy, but they are great headphones with high-quality sound. If you're willing to spend a little more, the Audio-Technica ATH-M30x headphones will cost around $70. They are designed for studio mixing and recording, so you'll have a professional grade set of headphones without breaking the bank. Probably as high as you want to go, the Sennheiser HD 558 will cost $100 and possesses an internal sound reflector that ensures you are getting very-high-quality sound in each ear. Sennheiser has consistently been one of the best headphone manufacturers out there, but often slips under the radar with names like Bose and Sony in the market.

Recording

In this section I will cover the basics of recording your podcast. I will examine recording to an iPad and a mobile device as well as a PC. The important thing to remember is that recording a podcast can be as simple as you want it to be. It depends on what you are hoping to produce. To get started, you might want to record something fast and simple and gradually move into the more complicated tools. Whatever you decide, ensure the teens you are working with are with you every step of the way, so you can learn together.

Recording to an iPad

Recording to an iPad is quick and easy.

Your first step will be to download GarageBand on your iPad. The good news is that GarageBand, although it never was going to break the bank, is now free for all iOS 7 users. To record in GarageBand, it's a good idea to have a set of Apple Earbuds with a microphone, which will cost around $16 on Amazon.

If you want to have multiple headphones connected to the iPad at once, you will need to purchase an adapter. The ONXE Splitter is popular and reliable; it will cost approximately $6.50. Once you have these things set up, it's time to launch your GarageBand app. Jeff Coon (2019) has provided several informative and clear steps in recording your podcast to an iPad in his blog post, "How to Set Up a Podcast: Clear Instructions for the Uninitiated":

1. Choose "New Song" by clicking the + symbol in the corner.
2. Choose "Audio Recorder" by swiping through the options until you see the microphone option.
3. Click the "Noise Gate" icon at the top left (plug icon), turn it "On" and set the slider to about 40%. This will help eliminate background noise.
4. Under "Settings" (wrench icon at the top right) turn off the "Metronome."
5. Expand the timeline by clicking the "+" button at the top right (under the question mark icon) and make sure "Automatic" is turned on.
6. Click "Record."
7. When finished recording, press the stop button and then choose "Dry" from the audio settings.
8. To see your audio timeline, press the timeline icon (to the right of the little microphone icon in the top menu bar). This is where you can add additional audio tracks before finalizing this editing session.

It's really as simple as that when it comes to recording a podcast on an iPad.

Recording on a Mobile Device

It's very simple to record a podcast on your phone. One way to do it is to use the built-in Voice Memo app (usually found in Utilities). You can record good-quality audio on this app, so it might be the perfect place to start. To get started:

1. Open the Voice Memo app on your iPhone or Android device.
2. Tap the red recording button to start recording the podcast. Tap it again to stop the recording.
3. Tap "Done" when you've finished recording.
4. Give the episode a name and tap "Save."

You're done! You've just recorded a podcast on your phone. If you want to do some simple editing and trimming, it's fairly simple. Open up your Voice Memo app again:

1. Choose the recording you want to edit.
2. Tap the three lines button on the bottom left of your screen and tap "Edit Recording."
3. Tap the trim button (it looks like a box) in the top right of the screen, and move the lines around to indicated where you want to trim the podcast.
4. Tap "Trim" and then tap "Save."

If you want to share your episode, it's also fairly easy. In the Voice Memo app, simply tap the three lines button in the bottom left again and tap "Share." If you'd like to email it to yourself, tap the "mail" button and enter the email address you'd like to send it to. Voice Memo converts your audio file into an "m4A," which is a very compatible file for any audio player around.

There are tons of different apps out there to use when it comes to recording a podcast on a mobile device. One that is really easy to use is the Anchor app, which is compatible with both Apple and Android devices. It's a simple way to create your own podcast on the go and on the cheap. It allows you to record audio files directly onto your phone and publish your podcast in only a few easy steps. It stands out from other apps because it's absolutely free.

It's designed for beginners, which is another plus. Tap the green "Get Started" button to create an account. You can do this on a PC or Mac if it's easier, and then transfer over to the mobile app to start actually recording. On the website, click "Settings," and on the right you'll see a space for your podcast artwork or logo (more on that in Chapter 6), so ensure you upload that.

From here you can enter in your podcast name and description in addition to your Anchor profile URL. In the "Author" field type in the name of your podcast team, and choose a podcast category.

From here, it's easy to get started with Anchor on your mobile device. The app starts recording when you hold your phone up to your ear, and it will cease the recording when you remove the phone from your ear. It also has the option of pushing the red "record" button and letting you hold your phone away from you. You can then listen back to your audio. Anchor has some basic editing functions, and you can "redo" your recording, but editing is very limited at this point.

Another cool aspect of Anchor is that it allows you to add some music to go underneath your voice as you record, as well as transitions to segment your podcast as you see fit. I think if you gave Anchor to your teens they would be off and running in no time, as it is very user friendly. You can download the free app, record your podcast, and have it on iTunes in a matter of minutes.

For your teens' purposes, publishing with Anchor will probably be the perfect fit. Your podcast will be branded by Anchor—something to keep in mind. They will, however, publish to the big names like iTunes and Spotify. This does mean that Anchor will "own" your podcast listing. If you're not concerned with that, then it won't be an issue.

If you do decide to record your podcast on your phone, here are some tips to consider: Know where your microphones are; they are typically located on the bottom of the phone, near where you'd speak on a "traditional" phone. There will probably be more near the cameras, so double-check that your fingers or cases are not blocking or covering the phone mics in any way.

Get close to the person or event that you are recording. When you're using your phone, other noises can really affect the quality of the audio, especially if you are outside and there is any kind of breeze. Getting as close to your subject as possible is key when recording on a mobile device. Also, put your phone on Airplane Mode before you start recording. This way, your recording won't be interrupted by the sound of an incoming message, phone call, or other notification.

Recording on a PC

Microphones

When recording on a PC, there are many platforms you can use. For our podcast, we regularly use Audacity. Audacity is a free program that is relatively easy to use. I had the students using it with ease after two sit-down sessions. It is free and intuitive and from my perspective has very few issues or bugs after almost two years of using it. You can download Audacity from www.audacityteam.org.

To use Audacity, connect your USB microphone to your laptop or computer. Ensure that you've got your mic selected from the device toolbar, which is a drop-down menu next to the microphone symbol in the top left.

Press the red button or "R" on your keyboard to start recording.

Press the Pause button or "P" on your keyboard to pause. Note: You cannot edit your podcast after you've paused it.

Press the Stop button or your spacebar to stop the recording. You can edit it after you've ended the recording.

I had my students record an intro first. With the microphone in the middle of the table in a quiet Library, they each took turns saying a part. It goes "Welcome to Booklings Chat / The Student Made Podcast from Glenthorne High School Library / Where We Interview Authors / And Discuss Our Favorite Books!" with each segment said by a different student.

It took us a few tries, as the giggles set in after a few bloopers, but after a while we got a really good recording down. Once you have your intro recorded, click "File" then "Export" then "Export as WAV." Give it a name and then ensure WAV is selected in the "Save As Type" field. A new menu will appear. From here you can add Artist Name, Track Title, Album Title, and other comments. You can choose to simply click "Ok" and leave the fields blank.

Next, we recorded an outro. This was "Thanks for listening! / If you'd like to be a guest on our show, email Mr. Maxwell at lml@glenthorne.sutton.sch.uk." Once we were done, we saved it following the same steps as above.

Then, it was time to record an actual podcast. The first few were simply the podcast team discussing what they were reading, what they thought about it, what they hoped to read next, or what books they were looking forward to. It was a simple, laid back 20 minutes of recording.

Recording Your Podcast

Recording Your Podcast on Skype

Our podcast team hasn't performed this particular task yet, but if you have a Skype account in your library or school and have a guest lined up to talk to, you can record the call through Skype and save it to your computer or mobile phone. Call recording can only be done when both parties are using Skype. Skype will also notify all parties that they are being recorded. They should already be aware of this, but Skype will let you know anyway.

Ensure you are using the latest version of Skype to record it for your podcast. Open Skype and go to the notifications symbol, and make sure you're on the most recent version.

You can also visit skype.com and click "Download Skype" to receive the latest version.

You'll now have to find your interviewee in Skype. You can open Skype and click "Search Skype" and type in the person's Skype handle, name, or email, and they should appear. When you select their name, you'll automatically be taken to a conversation window where you can "E-introduce" yourself. You'll only be able to send them ten messages until they accept your friend request.

Once they've accepted, select them and click on the telephone symbol to give them a call. You do not need to record a video call, although this is completely possible as well.

Once you've got your conversation rolling, all you need to do is click the "+" symbol in the bottom right of your Skype menu and then click "Start Recording." Once you've selected this, a small banner will appear at the top of the page with a red recording dot. It will provide a running timer and a button that says "Stop Recording."

Once your interview is over, you'll notice it appear in what looks like a video box in the right-hand conversation window. In the top right corner of the box are three dots. Click on them, and then click "Save to Downloads" or "Save File As," whichever you prefer. From here, you can open this file in an editing software like Audacity, which I will explain how to use below.

Editing Your Podcast in Audacity

Once you've got a podcast and you want to edit out any dead air or long "ummms" or false starts, it's really simple in Audacity. I want to stress again that there is such a thing as overediting. In the end, you want something that you and the teens are proud of, but don't pull your hair out over every single tiny defect. Have fun with editing, take out any glaring issues, but don't be a perfectionist.

In Audacity, press F1 to use the selection tool, or click on it on the menu. It's just to the right of the red record button and will say "Selection Tool" if you hover your cursor over it.

Once you have selected a section of the track you want to remove, press CTRL then X to delete it. If you've made a mistake and cut something you didn't want to, simply click "File" and then "Undo Cut" to restore the track.

To have multiple tracks running in Audacity, you need to shift them so that both tracks don't play simultaneously.

To do this, click "File" then "Import" then "Audio" and select the file you want, presumably the intro where the students introduce the podcast, telling your audience what it's all about.

Now follow the same steps above and import the actual podcast. You'll notice that both tracks will be situated one on top of the other, with the first track you imported on the top.

You need to move the bottom track to the end of the top track to ensure that the intro moves seamlessly into the actual interview or podcast.

To do this, press F5 or click on the "Time Shift Tool," which looks like two arrows facing opposite directions. Once you've selected this tool, left-click and hold down the button on your mouse while dragging the track to the right so that it reaches the end of the introduction. You'll know you've lined them up well when the perpendicular line between the two tracks is highlighted in yellow.

You'll have to press F1 to highlight the selection tool a few times to select the end of the intro and play it back a few times so that you've got a good transition. It might also be a good idea to zoom in to see your track close up so you can move them as close as possible. To do this, hold down CTRL and press the number 1 repeatedly to zoom in. If you want to zoom back out, or far enough to see all of your tracks from a larger distance, hold down CTRL and press the number 3.

Remember, if at any time you want to restore things the way you wanted them, simply click "File" and then "Undo."

You might also want to add a few effects to your track. The effect I rely on the most is the "Fade In" effect, as I find it creates a seamless transition between tracks.

To do this, press F2 or click on the selection tool and highlight the track you'd like to fade in. Then click "Effect" at the top and click "Fade In." You can click on this multiple times to make the fade in more pronounced. Play around with it, undoing anything you don't like.

Once you are happy with the intro and the actual podcast, upload the outro and do the same thing, move it with the time shift tool, create a fade in, adjust it so you are happy with its placement, and play it back.

There are many alternatives to Audacity; some are glossier and will do more tricks. However, in my opinion, Audacity gets the job done and is really easy to use. That said, here are few alternatives in case you think Audacity isn't for you:

Wavepad: It feels like Audacity on steroids, although it's still free like Audacity unless you are hoping to make money off of your recordings—then there is a cost. It has an easy to use interface, there is a lot of "stuff" on it, but like Audacity, it will get the job done and you'll be happy with the result. People have recommended Wavepad to me so much that I've provided below a quick tutorial on how to get started:

To record straight within Wavepad, download the latest version, open Wavepad, and click "New." If you have an external microphone hooked up to your computer, click "Options" and click the recording tab. Select the microphone you have installed from the device list. Select the microphone and then click the "Properties" button. From here you can adjust the levels on the microphone to make sure it is recording at the right volume. Click "Ok" to save any changes you may have made.

Then, simply click the record button at the bottom left of the screen. You're now ready to start talking, and you can click "Stop" when you're done. If you are finished recording and you notice that there is a lot of background noise on your recording, there are ways to reduce and remove them on Wavepad.

Open your recording, click the "Effects" button, and then click "Cleanup." Select "Noise Reduction" and then "Auto Spectral Subtraction." Under "Preset," click "Apply to Voice" and then click "Reduce Noise." Once the menu bar has completed its run, listen back to your recording to see if the noise in the background has been reduced. If there is still background noise getting under your skin, go back to the "Noise Reduction" menu and instead of "Auto Spectral Subtraction," click "Multi-band noise gating." Under "Preset" click "Reduce Hum and Hiss" and then "Reduce Noise." Using these two methods you should be able to remove a lot of background noise.

Need to trim your audio file in Wavepad? It's pretty easy to do, especially if you want to remove dead air from the beginning and end of your audio file. In Wavepad, click "Edit" and then "Trim" then click "Auto trim silence . . ." which will remove any dead air.

If you want to remove all silences before or after a different point in your podcast, simply select the point of reference in your file you want to work from. This will create a red line that runs from the top to the bottom of the file. Click "Edit" then "Trim" then either "Trim Start" to delete silences before your cursor or "Trim end" to trim everything after your cursor.

If you've found you've made a big mistake, don't panic; simply click "Undo" under the Home tab in Wavepad.

Wavousaur: This is another audio editor that's 100% free. The best thing about Wavosaur is that it allows you to work on multiple projects at once. Audacity lets you work on multiple tracks at once, as we've just seen, but not multiple projects. This is where Wavosaur goes above and beyond Audacity.

Oceanaudio: It's not complex in the slightest and is very simple and easy to use. You can load multiple tracks and edit them with ease. I would highly recommend Oceanaudio to anyone who finds Audacity's interface overwhelming. The great thing about it is that it works across any platform.

If you want to take your recordings to a slightly higher level or you're like our podcast team and occasionally do recordings on the road, you might want to branch out a little bit. We were very fortunate in that our podcast team won a grant worth over $600 to complement our idea. With this money we purchased a recorder that is portable and that you can record straight to an SD card if you want.

It's called the Zoom H6 Handy Recorder, and it will cost around $350. If you do decide to take the plunge and purchase a recording device to make your podcast slightly more professional, I can't recommend the H6 Handy Recorder enough. It looks intimidating, but it doesn't have to be. It can be used in a simple, straightforward way that provides high-quality recordings.

It comes with two microphone attachments, a windscreen, an SD card of its own, and batteries. It also has a USB charging cable in case you don't want to worry about the batteries dying out on you. It also has ports for four different microphones if you have multiple people recording during your podcast.

Your first step in setting up the H6 Recorder is to insert the SD card that comes with it. Turn it on by holding down the power button for a few seconds. If you're recording at a table with a group of people, you'll want to plug one of the mics in at the top of the H6 Recorder. The mic to use is the one that appears to look like two mics folded in on each other.

To turn the mics on, tap the "L" and "R" buttons that are located under the left dials on the recorder. From here, it's as simple as pressing the red record button and talking away. Once done, eject the SD card from the H6, and insert it into a laptop or computer to retrieve your files. These files can then be imported to a program like Garageband or Audacity to edit. The great thing about the H6 is its ability to house up to four different microphones, its portability, and the quality of the sound.

Our podcast team was very lucky to be invited to a library conference in Manchester, United Kingdom, where we interviewed over six authors throughout the course of one day. It was a long, exhausting, yet exhilarating day, which could not have happened without the H6. This was because we initially intended to only interview one or two authors and then enjoy the conference. However, once word got around that the students were interviewing people, more and more authors wanted to take part.

We interviewed a few with very short notice, and the H6 was perfect for this kind of atmosphere. It is small, lightweight, and can be set up in seconds.

Finding the right equipment can feel like you're in a maze. What's important to remember is that making a podcast doesn't have to be expensive. Start small, and get your team together and get something recorded—that's what matters. As you progress, you may feel like you want to develop the technology and up your game; however, there are several free apps like Anchor and Audacity or GarageBand that can get you well on your way to a regularly scheduled podcast.

Key Takeaways

- It doesn't have to break the bank to start a podcast. Free programs like Audacity or GarageBand can get you started for free and mics, and headphones can be purchased for a cheap price.
- Recording a podcast can also be done for free on several different apps on an iPhone or tablet.
- Using apps like Anchor allow you to upload your podcast easily and for free. It allows for music and attractive-looking branding.
- Podcast editors like Wavosaur and Oceanaudio are intuitive to use and either free or cheaply purchased. Take time to decide what will work best for your particular podcast and the students using it. Consider how often you will be publishing your podcast and how invested you want to be in editing and promoting it.

Chapter 4

Are You Sitting Down? Interview and Podcasting Tips

No matter how confident your students are, it can still be intimidating to sit down in front of a microphone and interview someone or even your peers. Here are a few tips to get you and your students started and hopefully on your way to making great podcasts.

Listen to Other Podcasts

There are tons of great podcasts out there to listen to. By having your group listen to great interviews, banter, and timing, it will give them an idea of how to proceed. The idea isn't to make them feel inadequate by listening to amazing broadcasters; it will hopefully provide some inspiration and get them excited about starting their own.

Here are some podcasts to check out:

How Stuff Works: A giant site full of different mini podcasts on subjects like science, history, technology, and much more.

Myths & Legends: Every Wednesday this great podcast gets to the bottom of well-known and obscure stories and myths throughout history. It has a unique pace and a great story-teller behind the microphone.

Nerdette: Described as a "safe space for nerding out," *Nerdette* provides insight into important social issues using celebrity interviews and rapid-fire pop culture references.

Radiolab: Covers everything from science to pop culture. It's about curiosity and understanding important topics, great for those students who just can't get enough information.

Practice

This rings true for both learning how to talk on the microphones and for learning the equipment. Book a few sessions where the students are taught how to use the equipment, and then let them play around with it. Perhaps one session on recording and another on editing their tracks will do.

Let the students start off interviewing themselves; it's important that the students decide on some kind of theme, but you'll find this will probably evolve over time. Once they have a handle on it, here are six tips that the students should keep in mind when they start their podcast:

1.   Enjoy yourself.

This type of thing usually goes at the end of lists, but I can't stress enough that if they aren't having fun or into it from the beginning, it will reflect back on to the recording. As mentioned in Chapter 1, it might take you some time to find your core group, or your podcast might have an ever-changing and evolving group of teens. Being able to record and publish what is essentially your own radio show from your library or classroom is such a cool experience, and you want to make the most of it and ensure everyone is on board and having fun.

2.   Be consistent.

This relates to several things. If you decide to record weekly, stick to that schedule. If you're going to go with every two weeks or even once a month, fine. It's probably a safe bet to say that the goal of a student-made podcast isn't to make tons of advertising money. If it is, then you should try to record once or even twice a week. Since podcasting is probably a very small but amazing aspect of your job, a slightly more relaxed schedule will work well. Whatever you choose, ensure the teens know that you are serious about it. Consistency relates to the length of the podcast as well. Our Booklings Chat episodes run from 20 to 25 minutes each, which, in my opinion, is perfect for student-led interviews with authors. Find a length that works with your teens, but try to keep each episode to roughly the same time.

3.   Get on those mics.

Whenever we have an author visit, I always assume they know how to use a microphone. I don't know why I assume this—they're writers, not professional speakers or broadcasters, for the most part. Once you have your teens trained on how to use the mics, you can gently remind any guests you might have how to best use one. To quote a phrase often used by one of my favorite interviewers, Marc Maron, who regularly asks his guests to "Get right up on those mics," always test your mics before you start. You'll see the levels moving up and down in green bars in Audacity, Garageband, or whichever recording program or device you have. Ensure the mics are at the right level; it should be near your chin and only around two inches away.

Speak directly into the microphone; try not to turn your head away from it. This is also tricky when you have animated speakers or teens; however, moving away from the microphone will reflect back onto the recording, and their voices will dip in and out. The important thing to remember is to stay consistent and to try and keep your mouth the same, close distance from the microphone throughout the recording.

If the teens have their questions or notes in front of them, ensure they don't rustle the paper or fidget with things at the table. I was surprised by how much the mics do pick up, and it is heartbreaking when you have a great podcast recorded only to find someone is tapping on the table or rustling a paper. Make sure they have everything out in front of them before they start, and try to have multiple pages laid out so there won't be the sound of them turning the page in the podcast as well.

4.   Keep it focused.

Again, this might take time, but if your podcast is about great, new, young adult fiction, it's important to keep the podcast focused on this topic. It's easy to stray from the road and veer into other topics, but if you want to keep the podcast tight and consistent, keeping teens on the right track will be important. If your goal is to generate new listeners with every episode, having a theme and sticking to it will ensure those listeners will come back time and time again. The reason why I've listened to some of my favorite podcasts for the past five years is because they've become like a familiar voice, and I know what I'm going to get each time I tune in. You will know your teens and understand what they want to discuss. I have an amazing team of students who run our podcast, but when we started I still gave them a gentle reminder that the podcast idea was to discuss young adult books and interview authors, and we were going to do our best to stick to that theme.

5.   Don't get swallowed by the editing.

I have gone over this a few times already, and discussed how to edit in Chapter 3, but it's important to edit out things that really stand out; however, it's equally important not to get obsessed with editing. Often, the mistakes that you notice won't be noticed by the listener, and if you're not careful you'll spend way too much time editing your podcast. To be honest, you'll never truly have a "perfect" recording. We've done podcasts when the fire alarm has gone off in the middle. That, of course, was a reason to start over and edit the giant ringing sound out. We've had people come into the library to use the photocopier, and I've decided to leave it in. In the end, I enjoyed the idea that the podcast was going on in a working library, and even though I had done my best to clear the area and book the space off, life happens. Find a groove you are happy to exist in, and go from there. Once your students become more confident, your need to edit will decrease.

6.   Watch the levels.

This is where having a handy member of the team is important. If I have two students interviewing an author, I always have a third student watching the levels either on Audacity or in the H6 Recorder. This is to ensure they don't stray into the red or go too low if someone is sitting too far from the microphone. Since we're comfortable with editing at this point, we have no problem pausing the recording and asking the guest to sit a little closer to the microphone so that we can pick up their voice. When students are interviewing, they might be nervous, in their own heads or fully concentrating on the questions. Having another set of eyes watching the levels has saved more than one podcast that we've recorded.

Interview Tips

As I'm writing this, the Booklings have interviewed twenty-one authors. It's been a fun and interesting journey, and here are a few subtips of things we've learned along the way.

1.   Confirm the time and date of the guest.

This is something that I take care of; I email the author a week in advance and then a day before just to check in. We confirm the time and approximately how long the interview will take. It's something that I occasionally forget to do, but it's very important.

2.   Test your equipment.

The day of the interview, we set everything up early and leave it up for the day. Either myself, my colleague in the library, or the students will test the equipment before the interview.

3. Don't pre-send questions.

This is important to me; I want the podcast to sound as conversational as possible. I've only had an author ask for present questions once, and we did adhere to this rule, but I prefer not to. It's not that the students are going to ask them any hard-hitting questions—it's the idea of keeping it natural that is crucial. If you know your teens, you won't have any concerns about the questions they are going to ask. If you're unsure, simply ask them to send them to you before the guest arrives.

4. Do some research.

In our case, this is simple: At least one of the students will read the book of that author beforehand and come up with a list of questions. If they are struggling to come with some, I will happily add to them. There are of course generic questions you can ask authors, but we try to avoid those if at all possible. However, listening back to our podcast I'm sure you'll hear the same questions repeated, and that's absolutely fine. It's important to do a little reading on who you are interviewing; this will not only avoid any embarrassing moments, but it will also increase the confidence level of the teens conducting the interview.

5. Welcome the guest.

This may seem obvious, and I thought it was until we did our first few podcasts. What was happening was the students were doing the intro "Welcome to Booklings Chat / I'm your host _____ / Today we've got author _____ _____ in / so tell us, what was it like . . .". And that's how it went, there was no "welcome to the show," no chance to breathe or to let the guest say hello. It wasn't that our students were being rude—it was nerves. They were in their own heads and rushing through what they thought they needed to get to. It reiterated the importance of doing a few test runs and ensuring the students take their time, let some air settle in between their words. Now we have a loosely scripted intro that we give students, ensuring that they welcome the guest and let them do some talking at the beginning. You want your guests to feel that they are just engaging in a natural conversation.

6.   Make your guest comfortable.

If your teens are nervous, then your guest will also be nervous. That said, nerves are a good thing. I'd much rather the students be nervous than bored. I'm very lucky in that our teen interviewers are all upbeat, curious people who genuinely appear to be grateful to be interviewing and doing the podcast. This all relates back to the first chapter on how important it is to find the right teens to do the job. If you have your questions pre-done and the teens have gone over them and you've had some time for the student to meet the guest beforehand, nerves should dissipate a little. Since we also conduct the interviews in the library, the space is familiar to the teens and hopefully makes them that much more comfortable as well.

7.   Listen.

This may not come naturally to your interviewers. They may be nervous and simply jump from one question to the next. I am extremely proud of our teens when I hear them reacting and responding to an author's response that isn't already written on their sheet of paper. When you listen to the interviewee's response, you'll understand where they are trying to go with the interview and what they're trying to get across. We've had a few really nice, poignant moments when the teens have sat back and let the author talk without stepping on their point just to get to the next question. The tendency at the beginning will be to rush, but over time their confidence will grow, and they will start to pull some really interesting ideas from their guests.

8.   Don't ask yes or no questions.

Have open-ended questions—lots of them. I ask the students to come up with at least fifteen questions, and that's usually more than enough for a 20–25 minute podcast. You will know how many works for the format you are comfortable with. The key is to have questions that allow the guest to wander a bit (but not too much). I've observed many podcasts that our teens have recorded, and in my opinion the best ones are where they've asked the author a question and he or she has rambled a little bit and gone off on somewhat of a tangent but revealed something that is genuine and human. The students can then learn to reel it back in; they will become really good at this but not right away. There is a definite art to interviewing someone (an art that has evaded me personally), but I love to see how great some of the teens have become at crafting an interview with the authors who visit our school.

Also, don't ask multiple questions at once; it will only confuse and derail the flow of the interview. If you don't get to every question, it's not the end of the world. If there's a burning question that the teen really wants to ask, ensure to bump it up to the front of the list.

Interviewing isn't as easy as it sounds. To be a good interviewer, you need to be a good listener. Have students practice on each other; ensure they allow space for the interviewee to "breathe" in between questions. Thinking on your feet and avoiding closed questions is crucial in creating a podcast that sounds natural and engaging to the listener.

Key Takeaways

- Listen to other podcasts before you start your own; hearing what other professionals are doing will help you decide on the format you want to use and how you want to structure your podcast.
- Stick to your schedule and keep it focused on what theme you have chosen. This will ensure your listeners will keep coming back for more as they will know what to expect.
- When interviewing guests, do some research on them before they arrive; don't pre-send them any questions unless they request it.
- Don't ask yes or no questions. Your goal with a podcast should be to create a conversation and making the guest comfortable; listening to what they have to say instead of simply jumping from one question to the next will ensure a smooth-running, engaging podcast.

Chapter 5

Uploading and Sharing
Your Podcast Effectively

To host our podcast, we use Soundcloud. Soundcloud allows you to upload three hours of free podcasts before they charge you a monthly fee. If you'd like unlimited upload hours, it will cost you $10 a month.

We use an unlimited pro account at our school so that we don't have to worry about using up the storage. Uploading a podcast to Soundcloud is fast and simple. Once you've created an account and a username (typically the name of the podcast), click "Upload" at the top right of the screen. Then click the orange "Choose a file to upload" button. From here you just need to find your podcast. With the Booklings' podcasts, I number them in the order that we do them and by the guests' first name. For example, our first podcast was with author Chris Riddell, so it was named "01_Riddell_Chris." You need to find a system that works for you, but for me, numbering has been the easiest way to go back and find the ones I need.

Once you've selected it, Soundcloud will immediately start to upload it. You'll see a message in the top right that says "Ready. Click Save to post this track." Before you post, you'll want to add a few things. First, the title of the track. Again, I follow the lead of my favorite podcasts and put them in order. For example, my first podcast is simply called "Episode #1: Chris Riddell." The key is to remain consistent and use the same system with every upload.

Next, choose a genre. Soundcloud is primarily based around music, so I chose "Custom" and simply called it a "Literary Podcast." You can then add tags; these are ways other people can find your work. I usually tag the author's name, Booklings Chat, podcast, and literary podcast, but you are welcome to do as many or as few as you like.

For description, I keep it short and simple. Something like "Celebrated author Chris Riddell sits down with The Booklings to talk art, politics, and the inspiration behind his books." Again, choose a short sentence or two that sums up the essence of that particular podcast.

Next, you'll need an image to add to the podcast. This will be the logo that will appear on the hosting service, bookmarks, or any other branding that you create. For many podcasts, the same brand or logo is on every track to keep it consistent. I recommend this because again, it will retain a certain level of professionalism in the minds of your listeners.

At Glenthorne, I ask the authors if they don't mind posing for a picture to use as the podcast image. We are fortunate that we have a poster from the American Library Association with David Bowie on it and the word "READ" written in bright red colors above his head. I ask every author who visits if they'd like to sign the poster and have their picture taken with their book.

This has maintained consistency in that the Bowie poster is always in the background, and listeners know it's in the library. It has created a ritual that belongs to the students and the podcast they create.

Sharing the Podcast

Once you have all of that info loaded up, it's time to hit "Save." From there, you can share your podcast to the world. If you click "Share," it will allow you to send a link to the podcast via Twitter, Facebook, Tumblr, Pinterest, or email. You can also click "Embed" to copy the HTML code to insert your podcast into your blog.

Since I have a blog that captures everything we do in the library (https://glenthornelrc.blogspot.com), I embed our podcasts and then share the link to my followers on Twitter. Embedding the podcast as HTML is quick and easy. I want to preface this by saying I know almost nothing about coding, so if I can do this, anyone can.

I use Blogger as my writing platform, but I will also cover how to embed it into Wordpress. In Soundcloud, click "Share" and then "Embed." Underneath the word "Code" you'll see a line of text; click on it once and copy it.

Now log into Blogger and click "New Post" like you normally would. Underneath the title of your blog you'll see two buttons, "Compose" and "HTML." Click "HTML" and simply paste your code. Click on "Compose" and you should see your podcast fully embedded in the post. From here you can also add tags, such as the name of the podcast, so you can easily find it in the future.

If you'd like to embed your podcast in a Wordpress article, simply copy the code in Soundcloud's embed page as described above. In Wordpress, click "Add New" to create a new post or "Posts" if you want to edit an existing one. Once within the page, click "Text" on the right-hand side of the page. Paste your code into the page and click "Update." Once you click back to "Visual" you should see your podcast embedded.

Creating a Profile Picture

There are a few things you'll want to do to make your Soundcloud page look attractive. First, you should make a banner.

This can be a photo or an image or anything you'd like. I like the idea of having the students create an image or take a photo that they want to use. Soundcloud's rule is that the banner should be 2,480 × 520 pixels. Otherwise it may appear blurry, distorted, or only showing a portion of what you want to show.

Next comes the profile picture. This is where I gave the students complete creative control. During one of our meetings, I had them all log in to Canva to create a design. If you haven't yet used Canva, I highly recommend it. It's a free graphic design site that allows you to use a wide variety of templates. There are paid elements to it, but for me, the free aspect of Canva is more than enough. I use Canva multiple times a week to create posters, Instagram post templates, bookmarks, newsletters, and more.

Canva requires you to create a free account and has several built-in designs, images, illustrations, and fonts that will really help you create a unique design.

Soundcloud requires that your profile picture be at least 1,000 × 1,000 pixels. That was the only rule I gave the students, other than the fact that it had to say Booklings Chat somewhere on it as well. It was a lot of fun watching them come up with their creations, and in the end I decided to rotate the images. Still, I think it's important to have one image that becomes familiar in the minds of your listeners.

If you're looking for an alternative to Soundcloud, here are some platforms that you might find useful:

PodBean: Podbean offers great podcast hosting services, and you can get going for free just like Soundcloud. With Podbean, you can upload up to five hours of content per month. You get really basic statistics with Podbean, but will have to upgrade to their $9/month plan to get a more in-depth analysis of your podcast.

Buzzsprout: Buzzsprout is a great way to get started in podcasting. The catch is that you only get two hours of free content, but if that's enough for you to give podcasting a try, it might be worth checking out. It also allows you to schedule your podcasts once you've got a rhythm down and want to publish your work at regular intervals.

Libsyn: Starting at $5/month, Libsyn is a very popular podcasting hosting service comparable to Soundcloud. They provide you between 50 and 1,500 MB of monthly storage and also have their own app.

Podomatic: You can try Podomatic for free or use one of their four different pricing plans. It has great social media sharing abilities that allow you to directly link to Twitter and Facebook if you're hoping to reach that market.

Simplecast: You can try Simplecast for two weeks for free to see if it's right for you. After that, it's $12/month and allows for unlimited plays and no caps on how much you upload. Like the others, it has great social media features embedded into its features.

Blubrry: What's great about Blubrry is their podcasting manual that provides loads of information on how to use their service. They too are $12/month, which gives you 100 MB of storage. You can also pay more for their unlimited plan. They have amazing customer service and are one of the most popular podcasting hosting services out there.

Alternatives to Canva

If you try Canva and decide it's not for you, there are many alternatives for you to try:

Easil: High-quality templates even with a free subscription. You don't pay extra for any of the extras that come with each template, which isn't always the case with Canva.

Stencil: If you're more focused on social media, Stencil will be a great place to start. It has an excellent bank of quotes that you can use to get your point across. It has a smaller number of templates, but it's perfect for quick, easy access to great design.

Snappa: Free subscription that allows five downloads per month, it's very similar to Canva and has all of the extras that you need to create a cool-looking design.

Pablo: If you want fast and easy, then give Pablo a try. It allows you to create images that are the perfect size for programs like Facebook, Instagram, and Pinterest. It also allows you to share directly to social media.

Whichever you try, it's a good idea to let the students create a logo that they are happy with. Let them experiment; let them have fun with it. If they're happy with it, that's the most important thing. There's nothing stopping you from rotating the logo to ensure everyone's design has a turn in the spotlight.

Uploading your podcast doesn't have to be intimidating. Using free hosting sites like SoundCloud make it an easy process with step-by-step instructions suitable to people who may feel timid around technology. Promoting your podcast using graphic design programs is essential in creating an image that stands out and represents your podcast accurately. Getting student input into this process is also very important in order to develop a product that students can see themselves in.

Key Takeaways

- SoundCloud is a cheap and easy way to upload, host, and archive your podcast. It provides a place for you to direct your listeners and has a free app that listeners can add to their mobile devices.
- You can also embed your podcast into your blog. Using blogging platforms like Blogger or Wordpress means you can easily create a space for your podcast. This works well if your school or library already has a website or blog that they use.
- Have your student team create a logo or profile pic for your podcast. This is something you can use to brand your podcast and use on any advertising when you promote it.
- There are countless free graphic design programs that can help you create an attractive-looking logo or profile pic. I recommend Canva because it's free and easy to use.

Chapter 6

Promoting Your Podcast

Promoting your podcast can be as simple as ensuring your school or local community is aware of it.

Bookmarks

As mentioned earlier, we initially created some bookmarks to promote the podcast. We used Canva to do this by creating a free Canva account, and choosing "Etsy Shop Cover" as our template, which turned out to be a nice size for a bookmark. From there, you have two sides to create. We included the name of the podcast, the library's social media information, a shortened link to the podcast, and some quotes from authors scattered around it. The student library assistants are also members of the podcast team when it comes to promotion. They sit at the desk and check books in and out, among a million other duties. When a book is checked out, they can give students a free bookmark with the podcast information on it.

Staff Meetings

We have two staff briefings every week, one on Wednesday and one on Friday, and both go from 8:15 to 8:30 am. In the past I've used these times to have students come in and promote new events and activities. It's a perfect opportunity to have one of the podcast teens speak to all of our staff members and highlight the fact that they've started a podcast. A teacher might want to be a guest or assist, and it's all about getting the word out there. As long as you have permission to do so, it's beneficial to everyone involved. I've also asked our head teacher if I could use a space in the staff room to promote library events. He thought it was a great idea, so that space is used to highlight the podcast, using the artwork that the students created. It's in an area that sees a fair amount of traffic and has drawn a lot of attention.

Wait to Launch

Before you launch your podcast, ensure you have between three and five episodes already published. This way, your listeners won't have to wait around for the next one if only one episode is available. If you have more than five ready, that's even better. Depending on how long you decide your podcast should be, it's important to have several in the bank, ready to go.

Create Promotional Materials

Once you have a few episodes recorded, you can use them to promote your work. Once again, Canva or a program similar to Canva will work wonders. You can create a social media template, take a quote from a guest, student, or teacher who sat down with you on your podcast, and turn it into attractive promotional material. You can then share these on social media or make posters to put around the library and school. On the template, you can describe the podcast a little bit and provide a link or even a QR code if applicable.

Social Media

If you have permission from your school administrator to operate social media accounts, it's a good idea to create a Twitter, Instagram, Snapchat, Facebook, or whichever apps are popular to promote the podcast. That said, only use social media tools that you feel comfortable with and that you have time to do. The last thing you want to do is feel swamped or overloaded because you can't keep up with new social media accounts. For Booklings Chat, I promote it on Twitter and Instagram, but I did not create a separate account just for the podcast. My professional Twitter and Instagram keep me busy enough.

If you do use social media, it's important to incorporate hashtags into your tweets, especially when you promote the podcast. There are many reasons to use a hashtag, but one reason is to increase engagement and awareness of your podcast. Accounts that use a hashtag can see up to a 50% increase in engagement compared to those who do not use them, according to the blog post "Best Practices for Journalists" by Mark S. Luckie in 2012.

If you are consistent in using a hashtag, your fans will be able to follow it and keep up to date on every post. For instance, we use #BooklingsChat, which is the name of our podcast, every time we promote or publish one of our interviews. This can be used across any social media platform, not just Twitter.

It's a very good idea to create your own hashtag for your podcast. It ensures that your followers can remember you and access your material much easier. A few things to remember when creating your own hashtag: They should be easy to remember and fairly short. They should match whatever it is you are trying to promote, whether it's the podcast name itself or your school or public library or whatever. They also need to be unique, which is a challenge, but you've probably got a group full of hashtag experts on your hands. Ask your teens to come up with some, brainstorm, and see which ones roll off the tongue and which ones sound clunky. Don't get too complex, and don't worry about trying to be too clever or funny. You won't win anyone over with these kinds of hashtags; be direct and to the point and people will follow it.

When you do decide on a hashtag, ensure you have checked your spelling before you post. This isn't the end of the world but can cause confusion or frustration, especially if you are copying them from another source. This leads me on to my next point: It can save you a lot of time and effort if you have a set list of hashtags already written down that you can simply copy and paste into your posts. This will ensure consistency and make your life easier. For example, I use an iPhone to post most of my Twitter and Instagram messages. In the phone's built-in Notes app, I write my hashtags out. When it comes time to post, I open the note with the hashtags on it, copy it, and then paste it into my Instagram or Twitter feed.

Before you go live with your hashtag, check on all social media accounts to make sure someone else isn't already using it in a way that will make it look like you are simply riding their coattails. Also, ensure that your hashtag doesn't have some extra meaning in the social media or online world. The Twittersphere will pick up on this immediately if there is, and you'll find yourself having to go back to the drawing board.

You aren't limited to creating your own hashtags, either. It's a good idea to use other hashtags that are already heavily used in order to incorporate yourself into the audience who regularly use them.

It's also important to know how many hashtags to use. This can vary across different platforms. With a program like Facebook, it's thought that you only need one or two hashtags to reach a wider audience. With Instagram, you can have up to thirty hashtags, and these can be hidden in your posts, so you don't need to worry about overwhelming your audience. You can use as many hashtags as you can fit on Twitter, but typically, people tend to use only one or two hashtags.

For the podcast, I use several general interest hashtags and more specific ones including: #EdChat, #EduChat, #Edtech, #ELearning, and #Podcasting, to name a few.

The website Wabasabi has listed one hundred educational hashtags to use, and the full list can be accessed here: https://www.wabisabilearning.com/blog/100-education-hashtags-educators (2018). Using and following preexisting hashtags is a great way to keep up with what others are doing and gaining more followers.

I highly recommend using the program Tweetdeck to follow hashtags and schedule your tweets. Tweetdeck is free and very simple to use. You can log into it just like you'd log into your regular Twitter account. Within Tweetdeck you can schedule your posts to make sure they are hitting your audience's timeline at the best time, check your notifications and messages easily, and create new columns that follow a specific hashtag.

For example, let's say you're interested in making a column for #EduTech because you were interested in how other teachers, librarians, and educators were using technology to reach their students. Within Tweetdeck, you'd simply click the magnifying glass symbol in the top left of your screen. Now search for #edtech or whatever hashtag you'd like and press Return. That's it—Tweetdeck will create a new column for that hashtag. You can then move your column to anywhere on your Tweetdeck interface.

If you have found a specific Twitter user that you'd like to create a column for because you'd be interested in ensuring you do not miss out on anything that they tweet, simply click the "+" symbol at the bottom left of the screen. From there, click "User," and in the new menu that pops up, type in the user's Twitter handle. Again, a new column will appear, allowing you to follow their Tweets. It might be a good idea to create a column for your own hashtag for your podcast.

The important thing to remember is that there's no real telling what kind of hashtag will take off, and if yours doesn't, it doesn't matter. I suggest ensuring the teens have their say on which hashtag to come up with, and let them have fun with it. If you create something unique and interesting and keep it consistent, that's all that really matters.

Add Your Podcast to iTunes

To add your podcast to iTunes, you'll need to find your podcast's RSS feed URL. RSS stands for "Really Simple Syndication. It is a way to easily distribute your podcast and update listeners when a new episode has been launched. In Soundcloud, click the ellipse symbol in the top right of the screen once you've logged in, and then click "Settings." Click "Content" and you'll see the RSS feed URL. Copy this link and then go to the iTunes Store.

Open iTunes, go to the store, click the menu at the top left, and select "Podcasts." In the right-hand menu click "Submit a Podcast." It will take you to the Apple podcast connect page, and it will ask you for your Apple ID and Password. Once you've signed in, go to the upper left-hand corner, sign in, and click the "+" symbol. Paste your RSS URL into the empty field and click "Validate."

Interact with Like-Minded People

This all depends on what your podcast is about. If you decide to launch a social media campaign around your podcast, this also becomes much easier. For us, interviewing authors and talking about books means we interact with authors and talk about books on social media. We don't constantly spam people, begging them to check out the podcast. We Tweet it out once or twice after a new episode is live, tagging the author and sometimes the publishing company on Twitter and Instagram, and then we go about our day.

Social media is a two-way street; everyone is looking for attention in some form or another. It's important to give others positive attention in the field you are podcasting in, and you as the podcast manager or administrator might get a lot of out of it by meeting interesting people and learning more about your teens' topic than you thought you would.

Transcribe Your Podcast

I'll be honest, this isn't something I've done before, but I love the idea of having the students write out the podcast from start to finish. I can see loads of benefits. On the face of it, it's simply good writing practice. Teens will find out that transcribing audio isn't as tedious and difficult as it sounds, and it's actually quite easy to do.

Transcribing your podcast is also keeping in mind any fans who may have challenges with hearing, as it shows you are aware that not everyone has the luxury of hearing that many take for granted on a daily basis.

Transcribing can also be a great marketing tool. Teens can create a blog post of sorts to advertise it, letting those in the library or school read through it at their leisure. It's also an amazing reference tool to go back and see what questions you've asked guests. Has your team been asking the same questions over and over again for different guests? A transcript will help them shake things up a little bit. This refers only to the interview style of podcast but would also benefit almost any other style. Going back over and reading how you've interacted with your peers or even with just talking solo can help build confidence and create better speakers and presenters.

A transcript also provides the potential listener a guide of sorts as to what each episode is about. They might skim through the first few paragraphs and decide it's not for them or decide it sounds like a really enjoyable listen. Either way it will help create a strong relationship with your listeners and let them know that you're serious about this podcasting business.

Promoting your podcast well can create a strong listenership that will stay with you and your teen podcasters. Using graphic design programs, word of mouth, bookmarks, and social media will ensure your podcast is marketed to the right audience. Uploading your podcast to iTunes will generate even more listeners. As always, having student involvement and input in this process is vital.

Key Takeaways

- Have your team promote your podcast by creating bookmarks, visiting staff meetings, and using social media if it's allowed in your school. The idea is to get everyone on board, listening and engaging with your podcast.
- Adding your podcast to iTunes makes it much more accessible. iTunes is by far the most popular place to find podcasts; having a presence there will result in higher listenership.
- Transcribing your podcast is great practice for your teens; it provides the listener with a guide to what the episodes are about and allows the students to build on their interviewing and listening skills.

Chapter 7

Activities to Podcast about in Your Library

If you decide to run a podcast from your library that is based primarily on covering events, interviewing other students, and promoting library programs throughout the school, there are many different events out there to podcast on. In this chapter I'm going to provide a few examples of "big" events in the school that your team could cover. Podcasting about them early on could be an amazing way to promote them, build interest, and increase participation.

Book Award

One of my favorite long-running activities to run in the library is our in-house Book Award, which is appropriately named The Bookling. In early October of every year we create a longlist of seventeen books, and by November we've narrowed these down to six books. We create this list through student-borrowing stats, word of mouth, and surveys we conduct in the library. The only rule is that the books have to be published in the year that we choose the winner of the Book Award. For example, if we launch the longlist in October 2020, all of those books on the list will have been published in January 2020 or later. I also do my best to ensure that these books are ones that are great but may have fallen under the radar a little bit, or they might be by debut authors. I have nothing against Harry Potter or *Diary of a Wimpy Kid,* but almost every child in our school knows those books. I want to introduce students to new, exciting books that will hopefully get them hooked and coming back for more. Having a podcast interact with students on which books they hope get longlisted or which books from the shortlist are their favorite to win would be a fantastic way to promote this program.

Once the shortlist is created, I do my best to purchase multiple copies of the books. I try for five or six copies of each. This is not always possible on everyone's budget, so choose whichever number works for you. If it's two copies of each book, go for two. You may decide to narrow the shortlist to four books so you can buy more copies. Whatever works best, the point is to get new books into the hands of students, getting them reading and getting a discussion going.

We start contacting the authors to congratulate them. I usually do this via Twitter, Instagram, and email. I then start looking for ways to bring them into the school, either in person or via Skype.

Again, here's a great opportunity to interview some authors for the podcast. We've already looked at ways to record a podcast over Skype, which is by far the most convenient and cost-efficient way to conduct an author visit. The podcast team could either record the author's interaction with students in the library or classroom (with everyone's permission of course) or ask the author to set aside 20 minutes for a separate interview with just the podcast team.

In addition, the podcast team could interview other students on what they thought of the visit, reflecting on their experience and what they took away from it.

As part of the Book Award, each podcast episode could be labeled as such and made into a series to build attention around the events and to promote them. Publishing an interview with an author and sharing it on social media, as well as tagging the author and their publishers, will do a lot for your Book Award.

I also bring staff to the library to promote the Book Award. Like I do with bringing in teens to start the podcast, I use food. I typically do this event after school in the library using homemade brownies, coffee, tea, and Krispy Kreme doughnuts if I really want to pull out the big guns.

Staff are provided with a flyer, which I place in their boxes a few weeks before the event. I then advertise it in the staff bulletin, speak about it in staff briefings, and send out one email reminder. This is a several-pronged approach to staff involvement. Every staff member who comes in is provided a library card. Many staff (especially new ones) are surprised to find that they are allowed to borrow books from the library, thinking it was only open to the students. Staff are signed up for the library and encouraged to borrow the Book Award books or any other book they might want.

The podcast team are also in attendance, conducting book talks on the Book Award books (most of the podcast team are in our book club so this works well for us) and hopefully interviewing teachers. It is important to ask permission beforehand to see if any teachers would be interested in being interviewed and if so, they can either set aside some time, even if it's only 10 minutes to be interviewed after the event, or it could be done during the event itself.

Students could ask teachers about the Book Award books, which ones they are hoping to read or what kinds of books they like to read in general. The key is to try and make it sound conversational and informal. It would be a great way for students to see teachers in a different light and to create even more of a buzz around the Book Award.

In the first week of March, we have the award ceremony. I live-tweet the event using a hashtag that is specific to the event (#TheBookling, to make it similar to The Oscars) and tag the authors as we go along. A few weeks prior to this, I survey over 500 students ages 11–12 using SurveyMonkey on the library's computers. I ask them to vote on their favorite cover, favorite blurb, and to read the first few pages of each book and decide which book hooks them the most.

This is another opportunity for the podcast team, interviewing students after they've completed the survey to find out which one is their favorite and to provide mini reviews of the ones that they've read.

On the day of the announcement, I try to bring in authors via Skype (or in person if the budget allows). We have a giant quiz related to all of the books, students sign up to take part, and I usually allow forty to fifty students in to have snacks, play the quiz, and enjoy the presentation. The winner of the quiz wins some free books and chocolate. It's an informal, fun atmosphere, and authors usually join in on Twitter. I will alert the authors to the date and time regularly as the big day approaches. Having the podcast team covering this event is a great way to promote it and makes excellent broadcasters out of your students.

Poem in Your Pocket Day

Every April, we run a Poem in Your Pocket Day in the Glenthorne Library. This is an idea taken from the poets.org website to celebrate National Poetry Day in April. I start by finding several short poems, five or six lines at the maximum. We print these out on library due-date slips, roll them up, and put them in every staff members' box. We also leave them out for students to pick up in the library when they're in during break, lunch, and before and after school.

I then visit assemblies and briefings to talk about our big poetry Open Mic. Staff are encouraged to come to the library and recite their poem (hopefully from memory). Students who are in the audience will then judge the teachers' performance. Students then get up and recite their own or perform their own original material.

In the past, we have also Skyped with poets during the day to do poetry workshops or bring poets in to do workshops in person. This event is a lot of fun and creates a lot of buzz around the school. It's also a great opportunity for the podcast team. They would be able to interview teachers about their poem, their favorite poetry, and record a "live" podcast of the poetry recitals. In this instance, the teens could act as reporters, commenting on the performances, relaying to their audience how well each teacher did and what the student reaction is. It would be a great lesson in editing but would make for a lively, fun listen.

Book Club Events

As I have mentioned previously in this guide, our podcast team is also made up primarily of our Book Club, so this is a perfect fit. However, even if your podcast teens don't make up the Book Club crew, there is nothing stopping them from covering the things that they do. There are a few book club events that would make interesting podcasts; for example, one of ours is our Carnegie Book Award meetings. Every year, seven middle grade and young adult books are chosen here in the United Kingdom to be shortlisted for the Carnegie Book Award. We don't run sessions the same way we do around our in-house Book Award, but we do ensure the students are reading them and discussing them. It's another great opportunity for the podcast team to interview the students and discuss these books themselves.

It may turn some of your reluctant readers into avid ones and get the books into new hands, which is the point, in the end. In addition, a published podcast that highlights these authors' work will go a long way in promoting your podcast and the books nominated. You could have the students record their book reviews as they progress, highlighting their favorites.

We also have a dedicated Manga Club at school that meets once a week. We watch anime, discuss our favorite manga, and take part in Japanese-inspired games and crafts. We also, occasionally, bring in an author or illustrator who specializes in manga/anime to conduct a workshop for the students. This is another amazing opportunity for students to interview the illustrator as well as the students on what their favorite manga are and why.

Our Book and Manga Club also take part in trips. Again, this is a perfect opportunity for members of the podcast team to get involved. We recently took our Manga Club to the British Museum to see the History of Manga exhibit. It was a fascinating time exploring the history of the genre that the students enjoy so much. For the podcast, teens could describe what the exhibit is displaying, gather student reactions and again, act as a roving reporter of sorts.

The topics to podcast about are almost limitless. If you know your teens and you give them space to create and discuss ideas, then they will generate their own ideas. It is crucial that the teens focus on a topic that they are passionate about; otherwise their apathy will shine through in the recording. Be consistent and allow the teens space to create, and the podcast will take off.

Key Takeaways

- Big events like book awards author events, poetry, or open mic events are great things to podcast about in your school library.
- Book club events can also be a great topic; having students discuss their favorite books, upcoming awards, and class trips can also be effective topics.

Conclusion

Podcasting with youth can be exhilarating, entertaining, educational, and hopefully, fun. As I have mentioned throughout this guide, podcasting can be as simple or as involved as you want it to be. What's important is that you give the teens a space to work in where they have fun, can be creative, and feel like they own the product they are creating. I hope this guide has provided some inspiration for you to get started on your journey to creating something great with the youth that you work with.

Bibliography

Coon, Jeff. 2019. "How to Set Up a Podcast: Clear Instructions for the Uninitiated." Accessed June 17, 2019. https://blog.hubspot.com/marketing/how-to-set-up-a-podcast-instructions-var.

GradeSlam. 2015. "Ways to Use Podcasts in the Classroom." Accessed May 15, 2019. https://blog.gradeslam.org/5-ways-to-use-podcasts-in-the-classroom.

Hudson, Chris. 2012. "Letting Teenagers Fail—Why It Matters." Accessed April 24, 2019. https://understandingteenagers.com.au/letting-teenagers-fail-why-it-matters.

Luckie, Mark S. 2012. "Best Practices for Journalists." Accessed April 12, 2019. https://blog.twitter.com/official/en_us/a/2012/best-practices-for-journalists.html.

Murray, Jacqui. 2019. "Technology in the Classroom: How, Why to Use Podcasts." Accessed June 4, 2019. https://www.teachhub.com/technology-classroom-how-why-use-podcasts.

Prangley, Charli. 2017. "6 Popular Podcast Formats: Which One Is Right for You?" Accessed June 10, 2019. https://convertkit.com/podcast-formats.

Wabasabi. 2018. "The Best 100 Education Hashtags for All Educators on Twitter." Accessed May 20, 2019. https://www.wabisabilearning.com/blog/100-education-hashtags-educators.

Index

About the Author

LUCAS MAXWELL is the librarian at Glenthorne High School in London, United Kingdom. He writes for *Book Riot* and is a contributor to *The School Librarian.* In 2017 he was named the UK's School Librarian of the Year by the School Library Association.